Not One Dry Eye

SHARON DIGGS

PAGE PUBLISHING, INC.
New York, NY

First originally published by Page Publishing, Inc. 2018

ISBN 978-1-64138-770-5 (Paperback)
ISBN 978-1-64138-772-9 (Digital)

Printed in the United States of America

A Compliment Will Do

A compliment will do
The caution of you
Warm dark tall
What a remarkable dude
Cut just right
In places receptive
Of sight to honor
You're a good specimen
She would say
Strong one here
Who can take his place
Careful about that company
You so secretly keep
Yes I been watching
For maybe a week
Got you on radar
Took my time
Ripe now for the testing
Fill my glass
Lest I thirst for more
A compliment will do
The respect you choose
Take the ball down the court
Run with style and grace
Got something on your mind you say
Let your voice be heard
Shout it heaven high
I heard your style ringing
Like American apple pie
Your kind is so feared

For so many years
Boats will float and smoke will choke
Swim it without that fear
The channel fowl
We go from coast to coast
No I don't care
Won't cut my hair
Ask me if I'm lying
A giant in stature
They sometimes say
I'm gentle and free
Communication let's see
Try to talk to me
Now keep it cool
Can we know each other
I won't start a fire
Don't shout
Don't shoot me now
Don't you be a coward
You just don't understand
You never meet my father
For if you did
You know it's royal
Now let's all hoop and holler
A compliment will do

Fake Friends

When you were two
You loved to play peek- a- boo
Family Chosen way for you to have fun
Got you past childhood dysfunction
Life couldn't get better
But now you're twenty two
With too much world for you
Sometimes you're happy
Sometimes you're sad
Pain in those trouble spots
Stress out and feeling blue
Started that game again
Enhanced peek- a- boo
The Ammunition got real
Doctor's prescription dispensary
Started popping them
Opioids was the chosen pills
Life changing thrills
Before you knew it
You jumped twenty years
Now Forty two
Don't got a clue
Never understood that phone call for you
Your mom asking about you taking them pills
Take too many you never gonna heal
Asked about those new friends
Got you out late
Have you had enough sleep
Your mind body and soul
Going to waste

Now she consider you needing help
For health and heart
You wouldn't listen
Popping pills played a part
Out with fake friends
Playing in the park
Woke up today
Just another twenty years
Wasted away
Sixty two now
Still loving that peek- a- boo
Time not to be trusted
Now it's too late
Can't warn you about your life
Your fate
All those demons on your plate
You consumed them all
Kept you up too late
Those fake friends of yours
Where are they now?
I'm at your wake
What a wasted life
Such potential but no Faith
Popping those pills
Opioids was not the way
The pain was the pill
Those lying friends
All ran away

Reckless

He walked like a gentleman
Sang like a fool
I was mesmerize
By the essence of Him
Caught by the collarbone
By the first slow dance we took
Yes you knew right then
I was totally unconditionally hooked
Reckless
You were reckless
You knew just how I felt
So tenderhearted I was
Icebergs felt will melt
Temperature was rising
Along with your attitude
Didn't give a care if anyone knew
Did what you wanted too
Sung that silly tune
Answered to no one
Not even your auntie shield
Your wealth and leisure
You left to your audience
But I was kept in secret
I wasn't a part of it
Played your games at will
On your terms not mine
Reckless
You were reckless
Behavior some type of royalty
Empty of dignity or power

You wore clothes right
Awkward at this hour
Trickery you were
With those silly
I'm so sorry flowers
I could care less
For your artless
Graceless sorrow
Reckless
You were reckless
Murdered our friendship
For fake friends of yours
They had no more interest
In you or your many toys
Embarrassing it is
To know I shared your fill
To know I shared your dill
Loved it when it happened
Now all is suddenly still

You Miss Me When I'm Gone

You miss me when I'm gone
Was Momma anthem song
Stay off my telephone
You miss me when I'm gone
Clean the dishes girl sweep the floor
You miss me when I'm gone
Come over sit with me
You miss me when I'm gone
Bake my favorite pie
You miss me when I'm gone
Boy don't talk to me that way
You miss me when I'm gone
Cut the grass trim that hedge
You miss me when I'm gone
Didn't hear from you yesterday
You miss me when I'm gone
It was my birthday the other day
You miss me when I'm gone
Your sister's kids getting on my nerves
You miss me when I'm gone
Boy stop going to jail you need to obey
You miss me when I'm gone
Come help me plant these flowers
You miss me when I'm gone
Don't you get mad at your momma
You miss me when I'm gone
I cooked Easter dinner today are you coming over
You miss me when I'm gone
I need someone to do my hair
You miss me when I'm gone

Stop slamming my doors that girl on crack or something
You miss me when I'm gone
Come put my curtains up
You miss me when I'm gone
Take me shopping with you
You miss me when I'm gone
The boy took all my CDs
You miss me when I'm gone
Your sister took my money from my purse
You miss me when I'm gone
Come dance with me my daughter
You miss me when I'm gone
Help me with this toilet it won't flush
You miss me when I'm gone
Why your grown kids can't visit me
You miss me when I'm gone
Got a taste for a gyro
You miss me when I'm gone
Can I see my new grandbaby
You miss me when I'm gone
Come get this disrespectful kid out of my house
You miss me when I'm gone
He broke my window once again
You miss me when I'm gone
He cuss me out and pushed me down
You miss me when I'm gone
Your sisters are fighting they won't stop
You miss me when I'm gone
They came over here to start some mess
You miss me when I'm gone
Listen to what your momma say
You miss me when I'm gone
You miss me when I'm gone

Desert

There I was face down in the sand
I raised my sorrowful head to glance
To nothing but desert land
From ear to ear tricked by fear
How in the hell did I get here
Contumacious indeed I be
Nothing no one my adversary
Who stands in this desert next to me
Only me in this empty heart that bleeds
Dread of adventurer
Cause gone wrong
This is how it feels
When one is alone
To have no parents upon this earth
Death robbed my home
I fool handedly said I would go on
I won't cry too much
So I felt no beginning no end
Abandoned and forsaken
Are friends soon found
Got to play those blues
Deserted the sound
So far away memories drown
Burden so heavy
One million pounds
But you can't see me
From beneath this frown
Hope so invisible

In this hot desert that surrounds
Need of deliverance here
You feel detached
From everything
And everyone
To nothing but desert

Kept His Eyes on Me

My last day at Gimbels
I was so anxious and nervous
About quitting my job
I sat on the bus had a seat to myself
I wondered why no one sat down
They stood in the Isle talking so loud
Kept passing me by my seat remain empty
Then I saw him
He got on the bus
Walked like a moving cloud
Had a beautiful smile
Floated on to me
His eyes glowed gloriously
He asked if he could sit next to me
I answered yes
He looked like an angel
My eyes stayed on him if to obey
Asked if I was having a wonderful nice day
I answered yes
Asked if I were on my way home
I answered yes
He just smiled as I tried
To peek at his hands
Which were so covered by the sleeve of his shirt
Asked if I could pull the bell
I answered yes
I couldn't take my eyes off of him
The entire time
It felt like forever
He just smile and said thank you have a nice day
The shirt he wore was heavenly white
Matching perfectly with

Everything else
His hair was in dreads
He was light complexion
He rose up without turning his head
Kept his eyes on me
Walked toward the front of the bus
Never saying a word
Just a wonderful smile on his face
Got to the step well
Went down
One
Two
Three disappeared
I looked around
I had no fear
Did anyone else see what I see
They kept on talking
Loud as can be
No one saw
Jesus but me
And Jesus kept his eyes on me

Sins of Family

Dark was the night
When Momma grab me
Put me in the car next to daddy
This place we can no longer live here you see
We be going up north
For better opportunity
Go where the people
At lease pretend to be
Neighbors and friends
Helpful if need
It was so scary
That night you see
Cause that truck we road
Was not ours to be
Took it from some total stranger
Don't even know his need
We drove off in the night
My family and me
Final destination
The north you see
My nerves so upset
Got the best of me
Stomach in knots
Wondering what would be
How many a curse shall fall upon us
Stole something didn't belong to us you see
Now daddy must figure out
Where will we live and eat
This is a pain from history
Take what you need

Don't ask questions, but please
Pardon my misconstrued family
Survival was all
The reason we flee
Got to pay back each misconception
Yes, yes, indeed
This be put on the backs of my siblings and me
My children, their children entire family
This curse this curse
Now was it all worth it
Too many years
Been paying for family sin
Give me my freedom
Give me my peace
Dear Lord
Let not my father's sin
Destroy me
I've been paying back enough you see
Free me Lord
Free me
For the sins of Family

My Spiritual Ear

I sat there holding your hand
You spoke to my soul
Telling me
Not to be sitting there
At the moment you will go
I looked at you
You spoke again
Hear what I say *now*!
I knew that voice
Even when your mouth did not move
You were still
Aware of my gift
You knew I could Hear with
My spiritual ear
Speak with a spiritual tongue
I didn't want you to go
But I knew this must be
If I am to see
God how you so work with me
I get no time to sleep
I sat there holding your hand
You spoke to my soul
Telling me
To hold on
Keep your sisters strong
Love them
Though they may be sometimes wrong
You said
I'm counting on you
Keep them together
To remember me

Soldier Girl

He asked me to
So I did
Soldier girl
Come here
Ready the forces
We need to clean up here
March into their camps
Spoil their treasures
Burn their tents
Sound the horns
Tell them you were sent
He asked me to
So I did
Soldier girl
Come here
Ready the reapers to obey
Send them out
Hurry before it's too late
Keep to the right
Stay Clear
Of the ovens in the south
Bring home a good harvest
He asked me to
So I did
Soldier girl
Come here
Ready my supper table
Put out my best china
Seat the guest
Prepare them for my entrance
My Glory is great
Welcome them home

Repentance

In due season
They disrobe
Change of color
Escape of mind
Giving birth to hope
And time
I reach for the strength
Of stronger arms
But for a moment
I'm not so all alone
I ease into the crowd
Camouflage of my faith
Are we friends or foe
Sharing of my heart
Now was that my mistake
What am I to do here
Did I awaken too late
Or was it too early
Maybe he was late
Personal Delay
Time is a measure
Of repentance
For God's sake
In due season

Rain drops
Form the beautiful lakes
Something so small
Becomes one big picture of us all
Are we one
The same energy
Of a collapsing sun
Grains of innocence
Deflecting for some
Or none at all
I am my own reason
I answer to one.

Dreamers

They say you should follow your dreams
But how can you
When your dreams run away
Torture each day
No rest
No peace
Fearful of the coming night
Sleepless for sure like always
Friends and family
Write you a nuisance
Repeated storms of heavenly bliss
They think you're sick
Your mind so weak
Rambling they say
Loose many friends this way
Your circle getting smaller today
How wonderful it would be
To have no dreams one night
Will it be normal
Or maybe a siesta mistake
Before the next fight
Dreamers have a hard life
Have too much to do

In this life
Not many clues
But you will be helpful
Too many souls
Many you never knew
Power of the mind
Who really knows
Its purpose
Or course its tracks
For display
The stars in heaven space
Might know

Is It Too Much

Life
Too much drama
So full of pain
Happiness sometimes
But it rains
So often
Can't help but
Wonder why why why
What's it all for
When we lay down
For the night
We pray pray pray
And try to sleep
For one night more
Some dream dreams
Of scary things
We hope never come true
But those with blessed
Gifts
Dream for years and years
Documented life events
We can't understand it or choose
Always in fear
Might dream of peace
But soon
Disaster and wreckage
No liberty
Joy is not found
In what happens
But what is
Life

Too much Drama
Give me one problem
At a time
One drop of rain
In the storm
Becomes a raging sea
My only home ruin
Now what's for me
Our tired bones
Can't rest here
For a short while
Bang! Bang!
Run and hide
If you wish
To see tomorrow
Another child hurt
Life cut short
Dead!
Grave visitations
One after the next
Smile and tears
We have a funeral
Next week
Life
Too much Drama

Feast

Now the weather was fair
There goes my hair
In need of repair
fix it or
Risk it
The chance the care
Listen here
To the pretty birds song
They sing sometimes stare
What's the story up there
Completion of this short visit
Must we all adhere
Finish this assignment
Handle it with care
Appointments are required
People ready yourselves
The end is coming soon
At a moment's chance
We are there
Colors brighter
Those golden stairs
Climb them now
Travel in pairs
Collected souls will all be there
Take a seat at
The chosen feast
Your name written
Upon the vessel fleet
Come into eternal peace
All that awaits is love complete
Welcome home children
Welcome home

Vessels

The potter's wheel
Still at work
Spinning out vessels
Broken again
How shall we mend
Diverge and purge those sins
Rise up these souls
Deliver them
Deliver them
Dress them in white
For church within
Keep it clean
Pictures at the end
Capture lives truth
Start here
Maybe just begin
Here we go
Let's tell this story again
You have he
You have she working it.
To a mysterious beat
Rhythm fine and neat
Balanced to defeat
Animosity and hate

No cheating keeping faith
Offspring from debate
Raise them up quick
Before it's too late
Teach them always
Guidance tribulation
The straight path
THE ONLY WAY
Weed the gardens everyday
Never never
To delay
Keeping pace to
To a melody of grace
This clay
Will reveal a true purpose
It knows the way
Built to rise
At a moment's cry
Hearing the voice
When the potter wheel
Spins no more

A Short While

Our existence
Is for just a moment
A short while
Shall we walk this rock
Celebrate its beauty
So awesome for some
Others go trashing
From crust to core
Majestic sequoia trees
Are magnificent glorious
Not many left
We were supposed to tend them
Do what we felt
How grand the canyon
Now that the water all left
Icebergs melting
Revealing what was kept
This rock giving up her secrets
Searching for some help
All stones rolling
Changing place fast
New landscapes forming
Time no more
Here comes the past
From the deep they come
Oceans give up her dead
Been sleeping a long time
Wake this moment comes fast
A short while

Almost done
Hope its summertime
Frigid winter is no fun
Water goes bad
Without some sun
No air to the breath we believe
School is in session
Many will deceive
Ears wide open
But can they hear
Our existence
Is for just a moment
Days turning to flight
We're out of here
Time no more
Now what shall we fear
Run to that grave
It awaits you my dear
Calling all
Having eyes
Having ears
Remorse is but little
When there are no peers
Listen with eyes
Our existence
Is for just a moment
This might be the year.

Lunch

Have you
Your last cup of brew
Roasted and toasted
Espresso for you
The right temperature
Too hot won't do
Held conversations
About the coming seasons garden
This awakening spring
Must plant the flowers
Pretty colors so bright
Birds will follow
Need those veggies
Mainly the collards
Cucumbers carrots
Onions and things
Squash and peppers
Not ones make you holler
Maybe go fishing out that new place
Bring home a big catch
Have a fish fry on Friday
Kids over tomorrow
Bake me that bird cake
You know I love so much
We been talking
Had no lunch
Cup up brew
Got cold
Wish I knew
It was your
Last hour

One Chance

We have but one chance
To be born
We have but one chance
To know why we were chosen for this world
We have but one chance
To become a friend
To love and hold another's hand
We have but one chance
We have but one chance
To acknowledge the creator of all
To ask about our call
To be taught
Lest we fall
We have but one chance
To walk through that open door
At an appointed time
TO answer questions, make plans
We have but one chance
To fulfill a dream let no one down
We have but one chance
TO say hello with a beautiful smile
Dance one Dance slow and close
With that special someone
You love the most
Stroll that beach

At sunset at least
We have but one chance
To live and build a better world
For others to heal give peace
Be for real give truth
Not steal from your heart or others
Love not fear
Make friends open ears
Let them near
We have but one chance.

I AM My Own

I am my own best friend
My own treasure of gold
A hurting soul
In a world gone cold
My life's not my own
I travel so long
A road so torn
Yet I go on
I am my own best friend
Love without end
I am forever a soldier
In this war against sin.

Respect

Do you know what respect is
Remember him who created the earth
Enlist your heart in the army of faith
Seek his wisdom everyday
Put him first in everything
Eat his bread
Carry your cross
Thanksgiving everyday
In every way.

Ready to Vote

They were ready to vote
Some were sheep
Some were goats
So few had hope
War was everywhere
Weep they did
For better days
Prayers were heard all over
But to whom?
What was their show of faith
What God had they chosen for grace
They were people
Lost in their ways
Some of the sheep
Had fallen asleep
And the goats of course
Were already at defeat
They were ready to vote
Some were sheep
Some were goats
Naked and hungry
So few could cope
Pain all around
No peace
So many so weak
Mustard seeds abound
What God had they chosen for the last day
They were ready
Same were sheep
Some were goats

Gone

All the things done
All the things said
Now did it really matter
Now that you're no more
Gone
We might have fought
You swung
Hit me like a ping pong
Maybe I bleed
But did it really matter
That time all
Gone
I still love you
I should have known
I would always love you
He formed me that way
People come
People stay
I only knew to obey
So dear momma
You were the best ever
You bore me
Carried me for nine
I asked God to bless your soul
Forgive you for all misconceptions
Joy with you was way greater
Then the unpleasant
He chose you to carry me
There must have been some great pleasure
So therefore Momma I give you heaven

I Am Pure

Just When I thought
It couldn't get worse
It got worse
I felt like
A lost something
In a prison of shame
I was all alone
Beaten down
Made to frown
Did not feel like a child
Of God
More like a child of smog
All turned grey
A sad delay
Lost in this world
Of null
My soul beaten
Unwanted mud
Discarded
No use
I was done
Forgotten
But still
I loved
Really loved
My God
Could not stop
Thinking of how
He had cared
For me
Protected me
Taught me

Kept me
How I longed
For my king
Free me
Free me
Please
My soul
Shouted

My God, my Lord
My soul retrieved
Lift me above
These troubled
Seas
I belong
To the house of truth
The house of peace
I am pure
I am

Life Is but a Little Bit Of You

Life is but a little bit of you
Just a taste
A small silver spoon
When the sun shines
Bright at noon
Warm and gentle
If the winds don't blow too soon
Life is but a little bit of you
A pinch of hope
When Moods stay a little cool
Joyful when the butterflies
Flutter at the moon
Life is but a little bit of you
Pure like an underground spring
Quenching your thirst
Of wisdom and truth
Life is but a little bit of you.

I'm Bleeding out Words

When Can I stop
I'm bleeding out words
But what for
Will anyone listen
Have you ears people
Can you hear
These bleeding words
Wake up
Time to gather
Call them all
You've known
This train's about to go
And it won't be returning
So get your one way ticket to day
Don't delay
I'm bleed out words
For your sakes
So stop sleeping
It's time to go home
People there is some one
Wanting you
Got the door wide open
I got the key to the door

Have you ears people
Can you hear
I know it's hard
And you've been tricked before
But have faith
This is your last chance
For your sakes
This trains about to go
And it won't be returning this way
So get your one way ticket today
Don't delay
I'm bleeding out words
I'm going to a place
Clean without spots of discord
No crime
Not time
No worries
Just that good wine.

Human Condition

Shall we talk about
The symptoms and signs
Of this Human condition
Will you see me in the dark
Of this night
Will your soul
Know my soul
Will your heart beat
At the same pace as my heart
Lord, what do you ask here
Can we do this
Will you hear my scream
In the middle of that storm
The one we be in day and night
Of this Human condition
Can we live
I know the years past
Seem like small moments in time
Many have gone
Many will come
Is this love
Just some disease

The one with no cure to be found
Of this human condition
This is terminal
I'm sure you know
No one can help us
Except we help ourselves
On this battlefield
There be just you and me
Every day passing
We still can't change this
This is where we be
Of this Human condition
Will you find me
Before I'm gone under
How much more of this
Can you or me take
This has got to stop

Spiritual Pill

Too much time to think
Why am I here
Just being filled
Oh this spiritual Pill
What power you have
You reach deep in my soul
Every inch of me
No space to spare
Starting to forget
To be human
But yes I'm still here
One breath in time
Caring for souls
Too lost to know
I'm working here
Always saving one or another
I've been so busy
Not sure if I was truly aware
This walk is so hard
But I must grow stronger
I have to complete my part
Fight to stay awake
Even if I'm the only one on this earth
Who knows
My tears will carry me on
Oh this spiritual pill
Just being filled
I'm here
I'm here
Don't ask me why
I'm here
I'm here
For just a little while

Holy Vessel

I came by
One month ago
To sit with momma
To share a word or two
From the Lord
To instruct my soul
What I had to do
To keep company
To comfort her
Share the Lords word
To wipe her tears
Sway away the fears
Soon Momma
There will be no more pain
No more hurt
No more hurt
It was hard to watch
So very hard to hear
But faith was near
The Lord comfort my ears
So I could stay with her
I waited to show her the way
To glory, Peace and heavenly bliss
I come by that day
One month ago
To sit with Momma
Sing her songs of laughter, love and
Spiritual hearing
With rivers of joy flowing in

What a miracle when she turned
To me with the most wonderful smile
And said you can do it!
She had moments of heaven
No longer afraid
Once lost but now found
She was on her last walk home
Her sweet savior
Was right on time
I was the vessel
To show momma the way home
Peace.

Can't Call You

This Christmas shall be so hard
I try to celebrate life
But all I keep thinking about
Is how much I miss you
I keep forgetting I can't call you up
To see what you're doing
I can't take your number
Out of my phone
I love to look at your name
On the phone
I pretend I can call you up
I know in time thus will cease
I hope
I pray God helps me
I got to go on
Missing you so much
Feeling like I didn't say something
Can't give you a present
Can't make you that Pecan Pie
You loved so much
Didn't get that last dance with you
But I did get you that straw hat
You always wanted
Momma you were love
You taught me so well
Gave me the best parts of you
Just as well

Story

Let her tell the story now
Repeat repeat
The sounds that ground
A soul so beaten down
No reason to be bound
But you leave
Keeping her where you please
The rainbows
Colored in black c white
Buckets of pain
At every sprout
The winds now blowing
I'm rolling down
Here I come
From this sad little town
Let her tell the story now
Listen
Listen
To what this sound shall bring
A pathway to life
Maybe pleasure shall spring

Riding this river
Of casual being
I shall sing
I shall sing
Bird of song
Melt this heart
Dress my soul;
Free it from these chains so long
Cover me with rain of Gold
I'm ready I'm ready
Finish this tune
A melody so sweet for a day in June
Let her tell the story now.

A True Tree

A true tree
Was once rooted
In the middle of a desert
Far from the sight that
The human eye could see
He waited many seasons
For the right storm to appear
To carry his seeds
Throughout the atmosphere
Human moods and feelings
Took change everywhere
Now life as it was known
Was at war
Death wanted to prevail
But the seeds
Were everywhere
The storms increased
As the humans mourn
For their rights
Some seeds grew
Great like the true tree
And bore fruit of
One two three
Roots deep

All Must

All the power
All must pray
That things promised
Won't come to delay
That time shall remain
Long enough to keep burning
Of candles bright
In the storms of the night
Full of fright
That hopelessness won't prevail
That the children will return home
All the power
All must pray
That those chosen to lead
Will do so
With haste
Without waste
That praise will increase
That God's will
Will be great
Without delay
His desires greater then all others
All people
Rise up quick
All the power
All must pray

Time

It was time
I heard the sound
A horn
A holy beat
My soul ready
For life
For peace
All around change
In the air
Harvest was ripe
Yes I grew tired
Weary
Strength all gone
but you were
Always by my side
It was time
I now knew
The reason for my life
Rise rise rise
The tide has come in
This be the last ride
It was time

Calvary Cross

How often do we wonder
Wonder about truth
How often do we question
Question about you
Closed hearts
Closed sight
Closed ears
Won't fight
We could spend
The rest of our lives lost
Not accepting the fact
That we were claimed
At the Calvary cross
So it's a shame
That we wanted to remain the same
The lost with sinful lives
Drinking poison
From broken vines
How often do we cry
Cry and ask why
How often are we shy
Shy about his grace
Stubborn children
With fears
Will never rise
Above the stars
They remain subdued
In a world of pain.

Schooled

He seduced me without skill
Empty empty
For real
Therefore and forevermore
I was given the gift of infinity
It would last forever
Enough to gather the wheat
That mater
Acid dip feather
Not smooth to tattered
My call would justify any weather
Schooled for the summer
Trued for the winter
Come spring not to fall
The best of them all
The secret weapon
The wonder of all
Come one
Come ya'll
It's time to gather
The gate is closing
It's for the better
Sound the horn
Shelter the home host
Collect collect
Count them up
Forget not one
Less there be trouble
We shall keep all that's called and given
Thank you.

From Dust TO Dawn

From dust to dawn
He worked
With his tool of love
He created his best
No matter what evil
Tried to work
His best
Rose up above the rest
Death no longer had power
His best
Now confessed a spirit
That lived
From dust to seed
Came his new Eve
And new Adam
Ready to obey
And on a very special day
Dust birth his way
His best
Now covered in a righteous flesh
From dust to dawn
He worked
With his tool of love
He created his best
And now
The crowns were ready
A new heaven and earth ready
Were now filled
From dust to dawn
His work was good.

A Blessing in Disguise

Once there traveled a boat to a new land
Its treasure in the cargo of man
Stolen from the mother land
Tears and blood would be their faith
Pain would fall like the rain
Cold and hard
So long was this treasure hidden
In disguise
Labor upon a strange land
Unrecognizable even unto ourselves
Reserved for a plan
Justified to destroy our enemy
In disguise
To oblige his every call
A weapon of truth
Ready for the last battle
Our intentions peace freedom, salvation
Slowly is the costume removed
Peel for pill
Until everything wonder is real
So long has this treasure been hidden
In disguise
The best secret for life
Hidden among the enemy
What great form, what love
A blessing in disguise
A hidden Jewel
Among thieves who wanted to rule
But hidden were the people
Of the holy breed
The chosen

My Best Friend

Of all the souls
I've guided out
Hers was the most painful
I've lost my momma
Gone home
Safe now
But I'm left alone
Maybe for a short while
Momma Momma
We will all be home
It's so hard being here
But I've got work to do
Must finish this work
She was my best friend
Spoke to her everyday
But she kept a secret from me
She was in more pain
Then anyone could wonder
Oh how I wish I could have
Been given the power
To take all the pain away
One more conversation
With my best friend
All is quiet now
How much I miss her
Could never tell her enough
How much I so loved her
My best friend
Momma I will always love you
I know your spirit is safe
And in a better place
Hard to accept

In this earthly place
Never want to forget
The lovely sound
Of your voice
I shall remember your touch
When you grabbed my hands
And held the tightly into yours
As I sat at your bed side
Oh my best friend
Now you're gone
Only from this time
I sometimes feel all alone
I kept telling you how much I loved you!
My beautiful momma
So special to me
I cry but not too much
I know you wouldn't want
That for me
I work hard everyday
To celebrate your life
Keeping the wonderful memories
Knowing that one day I'll see
You Again
My best friend

Duty of a Heart

If I know
A secret about you
Shall I tell
Or shall I safely keep it
Deep in my treasure well
For prophecy I've learned
Can't change one's faith
She can only warn
What may be in your wait
For daddy was caught
My soul was taught
Blade of that name did cut
That nasty dark lake
A moment too late
I could not stop it
Could not delay
For evil was in the way
Dues were due
Spiritual rules in order here
All the players must obey
If I could keep my love ones safe
Here for ever
Disillusion, disarray
Cook outs parties conversation hey
In wonderful weather
I would keep them here
Keep them near
Keep them safe
But every living thing
Has an appointed time
Rhythm rhyme in perfect
Chimes bells and fine wine

Give you change
For that Appointed hour
Filled to leave this place
Your mind
To choose my tower
For I live here
I abide in this space
Of for ever
If I knew momma
You would travel that soon
I would have sat on your porch
For one more afternoon or two
Laughed, dance a little more
Fewer family fights
Missing you so much more
Than I could or would wonder
Cry for me now
Cry for you too
I ponder this reason
Before a new moon
The season may be given
But the very time No
Faith I must have
You must have too
For God knows best
It does not matter
What I know about you
The moment
I will not know
When your rest
Or my rest
Is due

Forgive Me Father

Father I'm sorry
For the flesh I am
I'm sorry
For the hate I flame
You I always blame
I'm sorry
The faith
I abuse
The Hope
I loose
Father I'm sorry
For the years I cry
Accusing you of hurting me
I lie
Forgive me father
For closing my spiritual eye
TO the truth inside
Forgive me for sitting in the dark
Entertaining demons who lie
Father I'm sorry
For making you cry

Treasure Your Love

How is it to hurt
For those we've lost
Can't get them back
Oh how I want
This pain won't leave
But almost
But no
I feel it
Lonely place in my heart
Can't share that little part
No amount of time
Was enough for us
All the conversations in the world
Too short
Oh how I miss you
My tears are dry now
As the years' past

Memories come some pain go
I have one question
Or two
Who shall we miss the most
Or is it what?
Treasure your love
Protect it with care
For a season shall come
When it's not there
Those are the bad storms
Late in the night
Early in the day
If no sleep comes the night
For your love loss
Is the blanket one doesn't let go
Hold it tight
Treasure your love
More precious than gold.

Rays of Sunshine

Rays of sunshine
Warming down on me
My peanut butter shine
So fine indeed
I sparkle like gold
I twine with a twist of lime
On this skin of mine
Rays of sunshine
Warmth within me
My heart so blessed
My soul is free
I dazzle not frazzle
I have the spare key
Rays of sunshine
Come dance with me
Be my partner
Embrace my needs
Keep me
Cover me
Fill this hunger deep in me
Like brown honey toast off the Ivory Coast

Rays of sunshine
On this skin of mine
Satisfy this thirst
Harvest the grapes
Ready the wine
The taste so beautiful
A burst of healing
All over me
Rays of sunshine
Follow me home
Spray that magic
About my way
I travel home now

The Sound

You were gone so quickly
Not much time to say goodbye
Coming by to say it
Was so weird
Our conversation
Used very few words
We never mention
What was wrong
We danced around all the steps
Not to discuss what we
Knew was coming due
Each day I lost years
So many years with you
All I could say
Was I love you
I never knew a
Touch could hold
So much truth

You knew how much I cared
You probably knew
I was scared
I hope I didn't
Leave any clues
I would sit for hours
Because you matter
But the wait next to your bed
Grew harder every day
The sound of death so near
Was the hardest to bare
I stayed with you till the end
But that sound
Just won't leave
What an excruciating sound
It be.

Caged Spirit

I awaken
To this prison
Of fail memories
Time delay
Promised a future
With my only true
Soulmate
I am a caged spirit
About to unshackle
All faith
I count my moments
Of pain
With these written words
Of claim
To remind my self
That one more day
Might come
But those many mistakes
My soul all torn
Cause a wonder
Of why I was born
I am a caged spirit
Will I escape
This place
Such waste
My strength can't face
This rollercoaster ride
Of a soul displaced
Thrill me up and down
For maybe a simple crown
One day knowing a direction
The next it can't be found

I'm so lonely
In this prison
Of fail memories
Time delay
I cry tears of
No result
Some wet
Some dry
Many many wounded regrets
That I've forgotten
How to fly
I am that caged spirit
Spirit working on a prison break
Free free
This soul soon
Lest I never wake
Trap forever
No better weather
Sentenced like a fallen feather
Fall where I please
All focus gone away
Holding on by a string of hope
Casting out this last line o\to cope
This prison
All too real

Deep Funk

I'm in a deep funk
I can't rise up
Deep is this ocean
Hidden ship sunk
My soul id beaten up
Torn and triduum
My spirit cries
From known eye's bitten
But my tears are dry
The desert mostly empty
Of Water
When the sun shines high
Sad times for me
Hard life this has
Turned out to be
Have I any say
Have I any peace
The little love
I have
Quickly dissipates from me
I'm in a deep funk
This I truly know
And yet my soul
Cries out to me
Let's love God
Praise him
All I wanted to see
If I obey him
Will I remain free
But now bondage
Has taken me
I'm in a deep funk
Not a good place to be.

Gunman's Call

Bang bang panic
At that sound
Someone shooting
Got you down
In the streets
Run those silly clowns
Fighting for nothing
But something to frown
Bang bang panic
All around
School yard playing
Must hug the ground
Children all frighten
No innocence found
Grow up quickly
Can't hang around
No more fun
On the merry go round
Just 10 years old when she went down
Graveyard visit from all that sound
Bang bang panic
At the zoo
The animals all caged
They're not the danger
At least not for you
Hoodlums come a shooting
All in the wall
Better run fast
Escape you say
They just ruin family fun day
No peace here
Terror for lunch

Brown bag it for the scouts
Crazy is the season
These be the years
Sadness is the reasons
Bang bang panic
Fourth of July
Bondage is the fire work
No independence for y'all
Slavery to the sound
Of the gunman's call
Teenager gone but what was the cause?
Take back your freedom
Destroy the beach ball
Sunrise sunset
This might be your fall
Bang bang panic

The Tides

It gets me crazy
When I think about life
We woke up
We slept
We often times fight
It makes me wonder
Will we ever get it right
The years fly by
Day and night
We get a little bit older
But are we wiser
Now have we learned
Much in this hustle and bustle
Appreciation of life
Are we closer
To getting that sight
The vision that shows
If we've gotten it right
These moments of pride
Hope we haven't wasted precious time
Building up something
Changing minds with reason
Turning the tides
Waves that come in
Go back out with the why

Landscapes are different
But are they helpful
Are we understanding
Are we getting better
Learning to love
Still watching those birds
In the heavenly sky
We only need one dove
A sign to show
If we know
The tides

My Kite

I thank you for my heart
I thank you for the part
It plays in this daily meditation of you
I thank you for the thoughts
It keeps in reserve
When I'm empty and without
I thank you for conversations
Of manifestation of creations to come
I thank you for hope
Of better tomorrows
Quicker days
Slower nights
Wonderful memories sharing life
I thank you for my fight
To love despite
Disagreements dissatisfactions
Disrespectful little plights
I thank you for friends
Who mend with rough winds that bend
I thank you
I thank you

This Pen

I write down my pains
I bleed out this pen
I share my thoughts
With those who hear
Open up ears
Have no fear
These words are hard
But all must adhere
Understand me now
This allegiance to God
Support for the years
Follow the light
The details are here
Be fast and quick
The blood on this pen will stick
I write down my pains
Squeeze out every drop
Pop the bottle
Let it out
Press me for more
My heart forgives

Nothing from You

What shall I ask
I want nothing from you
Many people want it
Wanna go to heaven
What shall they do
They fear hell
Demons and devils
For the fail
I thought on this reason
I was not impressed
For I could care less
My sins were great
Therefore Hell was the right place
For all who were in such haste
The creator of all
I was concern for your sake
I wanted your seat to be true
Holy and ready for you
I wanted to honor you
Keep heaven perfect and true
I guess my love
Was pure after all
I want nothing from you
But I often cried
For who really deserved heaven
Truly you and a begotten son who died
Creator of souls
Who did no wrong
I want nothing from you.

Master Plan

His master plan
Gave me life
His love showed
Me how to heal
His grace called me
To stand still
His mercy
Gave me a reason to deal
With the ups and down's of life
My foolish pride
Sometimes tried to kill
My desire
To inspire
Souls to a higher sky
His master plan
Was the holy hand
That lifted me
Higher higher
Up from my deep funk
I was in
I was then in
The I don't wanna be
Place of sin
Now I am willing once more
To keep the peace
Finish the work
He started

This Roundabout

Driving down this street
Then here it comes
This roundabout
I don't like it
Got me going in circles
I'm dizzy here
Will you yield to me
Or dust keep going
Respect my rights
I'm right here
I've got the right away
But you don't like it
Suns in my face
But I still see you
Pupils may dilate
But I still got it
This roundabout
This roundabout
I don't like it
Driving too fast
Claim you didn't see it
My silver BMW
You just hit it
Drove me off the road
Now look at this
This big mess
For driving in circles
And shit
This round about
This round about
I don't like it.

Days of Night

All those days
I gave you everything
My soul spirit
Blood and tears
I have nothing left
I'm done
All gone
Why
Why I asked
I was so very young
Why was I chosen
To live this painful
Nightmare called life
The pain
I can't even write
With this pen
It can't be explained
All those days
Days of night
Lonely soul
Without wings for flight
Is there anyone like me
Just one I ask.

House

In this house in a house
Where the roof cries
the stairs throw me down
drive-bys
Kin-thieves on this unholy ground
Trash decor forevermore
Unleashed dogs come to seeker chores
The years a rage
dreams to stage
a life of discomfort to bare
Rise today rise
My way to an opera of duty faith
hear my heart
A drum to paint
Rose colored landscapes
This jungle range
Backbone pain
Come welcome me home
I will escape this funky debate
Reason I already cake
Savor the taste
honey chocolate
For God's sake

House for a Rose

There once was a man
Who built a house
Filled it with
His heart and dreams
Mahogany
Maple
Oak
To Start
Sapphires
Diamonds
Emeralds
That's right
Gold and silver
Just so tight
Cathedral ceilings
To every delight
Spiral stair cases
Everywhere
Oh what might
Secret rooms
All around

Greenhouse
Pool house
Shall I look for more
The next room
Better than the one before
Magnificent Kitchen
Royal by Sight
with cabinets and doors
like never
Ever seen
Let it all our room
Just scream and shout
for those who have means
or a way out
a house so built
To please a queen
for her
That woman
he would forever
Adore

Take flight

I Timescape
Take flight
travel through time
take flight
in time
in time of urgency
when called
by the Spirit

The Walk

I got caught up
In the physical
Mudslide of life
My soul had a need
To purge me
You see
Necessary to reach up
Near the lord
a closer walk was desired
a closer walk indeed
the pain has come
a road to such in need
pebbles of truth
Coming down on you and me
Rainbows of hope
Melt the hurt knew
a washed new day
fresh and cool
better days ahead
This is true
Wisdom a true teacher
a knowledge call
Hear her voice
You won't fall

True love knows

Rivers run best
from east to west
following the sun and moon
to reach its quest
over distant sands
and tree covered lands
this is the path true love knows
so gentle does she flow
when the heart of the river knows
what works best
keep her path clear
She moves to the
rhythm of life's test
Rivers run best
from east to west
down mountains
through valleys
Out to sea
her cycle never ends
her flow is forever
She brings forth life
from the desert sands
for true love always
Has pen arms and hands
ready to embrace
and meet every need

Long flight

What you say
What have I done
I fuss and cuss
because I'm not safe
I try to protect
My self
Shall I buy it
Myself
Oh, now that's a worth
quick!
I'm to blame
My only true love
it's you I say
who is not by my side
believe I'm alone
All buy it
Myself, yes, myself
hurt hurt hurt
is all I sing
was it my dream
All is not what it seem
I fell down hard
hit the floor
hard solid thing
it was
cold cold cold
my ears rang for days
I could not hear
My father's voice
oh so near
but I was covered

Masked in fear
afraid to love
no one to steer
come closer
come closer
all the way up here
I told you
you were welcome
had never to fear
I love you
for you
I love you
one clue
never stop talking
talking and walking
with you
I change the person
did you feel that wave
Now I'm talking
a father's way
I'm in you
you in me
we are one
the pain I see
got you up early
didn't know I would
I stayed close
you needed me most
your shanadakins
were worst
but I claimed
You first
My rose fruit burst
The sweet smell of you
of you
I say

yeah you didn't know
I cared so much
I read the soul
My mystery I keep
I know my sheep
strong or weak
your strength comes
from challenges and
complaint it feeds
a fussy baby
with rainbow paint
I love mine
don't you know
I keep mine
don't I show
I reap mine
don't you grow
I heal mine
don't you sow
been watching
yes yes you
for all this time
never leave you alone
not for one cry
tears I wipe
I treasure for life
a powerful act
sacred as a wife
I bleed it out
but most have not seen
one little girl
knew just what I meant
Joy came to me
a dove in flight
that's why I come
that faithful night

truth a spare
flying that kite
the breeze cooked
the wind
that holy night
soon
very
soon
no wonder why or what
for reasons so tight
I'm precise
I'm right
you gave the answer
I beheld the night
the beautiful reason
I've held you close
such a long
long flight

Still Alive

How much of you
is still alive
I was murdered
One
Two
Three lives ago
beaten down
forced to believe
I was a lie
Stupid girl
they say
with too many
dreams of buttercup flies

Song of Peace

My heart sings the song of peace
a melody for
the brokenhearted
the hopeless
the lost soul
he is with us
endure we do
all that is put before us
we are never alone
even when it feels
so lonely and cold
when we hear
no answer for us
his voice sometimes
makes no sound
when the pain is great
he whispers once again
so don't give up
he is our song of peace
our melody
he will never over look us
never skip
never skip
never beat us up

My heart sings the song of peace
a melody for
the weak
the hurt
the broken
allow him in
let him walk with us
for pain we will endure
for this is our gown of glory
the color of our story
we must wear our strips of pain
for he shall heal us
in the end
so hear this song of peace
for our souls
in the midst
of war against this life
know that we don't stand alone
for we have a true family
of love
he will deliver us
keep this melody around
don't give up
we gonna make it

One Way ticket

I'm on a holy cruise
I'm gonna enjoy the ride
this trip is a one-way ticket to life
I bought my ticket early
in my days
didn't wait for the rush
had time to pack my bags
haven't left out a thing
this expedition is for those who
love to love to love
if you know what I mean
must understand this feeling
so you can stroll with its healing
hope you got your ticket
'cause this ship
only has one more trip
ain't coming back again
if you will like to join me
on this wonderful cruise
you can't be scared to do
all that must be done
in the progress to be true
so make your way to
The holy gate
the horns about to blow
we about ready to close
the show
last call for tickets
so march this melody
with me

I wanna cry

I wanna cry
but if I did
I'll probably drown
for I cry
so many tears for you
but I'm gonna be alright
I just keep getting
caught up
in what you did for me
I didn't deserve such
a kind person like you
my place taker
you covered me
blessed me
and bought my freedom
so that I could see
I thank you
for allowing me to believe
in you
I wanna cry
but I'm gonna try
to keep your words inside of me
believe believe believe
and remember why
you so cared for me
no one has ever done so much for me
therefore I will abide

with whatever you
desire of me
I wanna cry
but if I did
I'll probably drown

No Mystery

It seems to me
That life is no mystery
it's full of hurt and pain
and untruthful history
Black and white
is not what I see
for I look upon
The heart
All that others don't see

Not one dry eye

I was stuck
but my heart
wanted to say
I was loss
in the scent of you
not gonna bathe
for even the
honeybees would stay
to play
love was first created
when one alone
allowed his heart to be touched
by a rose so sweet and alive
a moment so special
all the angels cried
not one dry eye
heaven opened her doors to life
from her windows
poured out blood and water
finally, he came
so beautiful
so perfect
so true rain comes when dew
Remember this we knew

Spring Cleaning

Cleaning out my heart
One Spring Morning
I came across some cobwebs
hidden down one lonely path
black widow spider
ready for a chance
I was quick
I got her out fast
dust dust dust
I was free at last

Fragile/ Handle with care

He gave us life
so fragile
sent his spirit
to keep it real
so handle with care
his words become truth
a light
in all our dark times
his messengers
did tell his way
his story
without delay
on time
to ensure faith
for repentance
to provide a place
for those who care
and chose to obey
he gave the life
of his only begotten son
so fragile so pure
so that we could know
handle with care
This precious Gift called life

Bloodriver

8, 10, 14
too young to die
bang bang
is all you hear
fighting over nothing
rushing to leave here
all you got is
death in the summertime
children can't play
life so short
got to be a better place
Bloodriver ruining the city over
running its banks
Contaminate the minds
of the young
so many
innocence gone
Children gotta grow strong
pick it up quick
no time to ponder or pick up sticks
bang bang
is the song of the city
hit the floor quick
or be the coroners pick
Bloodriver ruining the city over
running its banks
no love
what a pity

A Life be

What would a life be
if there were no dreams
how would you tell
your heart which direction to see
what would a home or love be
without wisdom
to float our ships out to sea
tunes for our melodies
colors for the bees to tease
what would a life be
without some mystery
a reason to build toward
a worthy deed
to understand why
love is a need
to want a child
to be blessed to conceive
share yourselves with others
in need
what would a life be
if there were no memories
no hope to seed
no reason to lead
what would a life be

My Heartbeat

In the sound of my heartbeat
I hear the cry of memories
stories to set the soul free
Answers to questions
of why we be
This drum tells a melody of hate
and why the eye doesn't see
special tone
with a spice we need
to melt hard hearts
and do righteous deeds
Man was lost
goes this story
trap in fear with his worries
Love was bound in this history
but righteousness
would return in this century
in the sound of my heartbeat
My soul heard all this
Answers to questions
of why we wish
for better days filled with bliss
a change of ways
Then this could exist

Brothers and Sisters

Brothers and Sisters
Keep the faith
the rain is about to start
cold nights ahead
hurtful words will be shed
for these are the last days
Brothers and Sisters
Mend your ways
repent and be saved
worry not for windy days
for storms come
in many ways
some wet some dry
open your eyes
look out and ask why
The stars few
The animals blue
so why are you lost
at what you should do
Brothers and sister
Move quick
don't watch a flick
get your drinks
before your vessel sinks
for you he picks
don't let his words
cause bitterness
he came
for you
The sick

A Labor of Love

A Labor of Love
A Labor because
She made love
so I could be
A Labor of Love
A Joy to be
She gave to me
The holy tea
A Labor of Love
A Labor of Love
A Labor because
She had a heart
A desire to see
What a miracle I would be
A Promise from God
A Prophecy
That only one special woman
was chosen to be
The Mother Who Labor
to set me free
A Labor of God's grace
A Labor of Love
a Labor of Peace
Thank you, Mom
'Cause you Labor for me

My Extraordinary/My Real

Remarkable was his sound
so sweet to my heart
a blessing for the ear
woke me up to be still
the touch ooh I still feel
Fantastic appeal
willing a grateful indeed
My Extraordinary
My real
your first kiss
Impressive
My soul believed
your love miraculous for me
greatness warmth to please
My extraordinary
my real
never a touch so tender
a whisper so pure
as his on my day of rebirth
revived for life once more
My Extraordinary
My real

My Twins

I had a little boy
who was so beautiful
full of grace
and a holy face
My little Angel
born too soon
taken home to the Father
for a peaceful place
a life so short
and yet so full
Will be missed by many
but surely by his twin
a little bigger boy
Just as beautiful
with much fight
to keep me with a smile
My number two Angel
born too soon

My Little One

My little one
At a new place
Not home yet
but so close
My heart sore
for the long wait
Peace so far
from my soul
My little one
O how I yearn
to have you home
its been so long
I've endured
this fear
come home soon
make it this soon
My little one
I see your face
hope I keep
to fill this space

The Color that be

The murex drizzle with gold
Yes I shall unfold
This truth the purpose
must be told
this is a story I know
because of the integument spirits
that dance about your soul
your resting place should hold
My invitation to come or go
I can't just snatch this plate
cause infestation, estimation
of expectation
your friends know the plan
of ashes that rise at his presence
delocalize, utterance concerning you
we are but vessels in his plan
of deliverance a soul
be freed man
tell me what purpose
What means
Shall I please
Will you give me the reason
The reason
is this treason

Maybe time doesn't shelter
or maybe believe or forget
does it matter
for knowledge
My college from above
I'm made sick here
My bones ache for more
The plan so great
my heartbeat breaks
it's so critical miscible
whom must I blame
if it's never done
too late

About the Author

Sharon Diggs is a spiritually gifted poet. She has enjoyed writing poetry for over twenty years, sharing her gift only with family and friends who have cherished her poems for their wonderful spirit-lifting, healing effects. She felt inspired to publish when, at her dying mother's bed side, her mother suddenly sat up in bed, smiled, and in her final audible voice, shouted, "You can do it." Sharon took these words to heart for her mother loved her poems. She knew it was time to share her gift. She resides in Milwaukee, Wisconsin, with her husband of thirty-one years, Gregory. They have seven children and four grandchildren. She loves Bible reading, writing and tending her garden.

CPSIA information can be obtained
at www.ICGtesting.com
Printed in the USA
FFOW03n0412040218
44849489-45010FF